ALL THE OTHER
PHIL THOMPSONS
ARE DEAD

BRIAN + DEBBIE:

HOPE YOU GET YER
FREEZIN ASSES
OUTA THERE SOON.

Phil

Acknowledgments
Several of these poems have appeared in *Such a Neat Idea, We People, Chezzetcook* (Wooden Anchor Press), *BS Poetry Journal, The Antigonish Review, Northern Writes, The Pottersfield Portfolio, Atlantic Advocate, The Halifax Herald, Yellowknifer The (Dalhousie) Gazette* and *Voices Down East* (Fourth Estate).
    Several of Phil's poems herein have been set to music by Pete Stokes, LightHouse Music, 13307 Pendicton St, Ford Washington MD 20744, USA. Tel/Fax 301 203-1686, LHMusic@juno.com

Cover photo © 1990 Joe Blades
Author photo © 1998 Jacob Thompson
Design and in-house editing by the publisher, Joe Blades
Printed and bound in Canada

The Publisher gratefully acknowledges the support of the Canada Council for the Arts and the New Brunswick Department of Economic Development, Tourism and Culture.

THE CANADA COUNCIL | LE CONSEIL DES ARTS
FOR THE ARTS | DU CANADA
SINCE 1957 | DEPUIS 1957

Canadian Cataloguing in Publication Data
Thompson, Phil, 1951-

    All the other Phil Thompsons are dead

    Poems.
    ISBN 1-896647-05-7

I. Title.

PS8589.H276A74 1999   C811'.54   C00-950093-7
PR9199.3.T65A74 1999

Broken Jaw Press
Box 596 Stn A
Fredericton NB E3B 5A6
Canada

tel / fax 506 454-5127
www.brokenjaw.com
jblades@nbnet.nb.ca

ALL THE OTHER PHIL THOMPSONS ARE DEAD

poems by
Phil Thompson

Fredericton • Canada

This book is dedicated to my sons

Daniel, Shawn & Jacob

*may you always keep music and poetry in your hearts
and have rowing, chopping wood, and sailing
to keep you strong and free*

CONTENTS

PREFACE

Island Man

Head in clouds, feet in water
sandals and black toenails
green, yellow and red rubber boots, floater jackets
his body is strong, lean, filled with history
the family DNA repeated

Lives are replayed and courage honoured
in mornings of coffee brewing, silence rising
Stories are embedded in tide times, charts
storm manoeuvres, ocean disasters
canoes on ice, rowboats waiting for repair

Island man is a patron of simplicity
a refashioned warrior who knows his truth
but forgets its source
in the straw houses of urban reality

Grounded in the rhythm of the tide
he is a journey man without a map
a word sculptor with no mould

One distant clock ticks quietly ...

There is a time to row, to empty rainbarrels
to cut and gather wood, secure boats on moorings
and monitor the sun's generosity

You could see
the colour of his eyes change
from green to brown
or gold
depends on the island shadows
and his poet's dialogue.

— Jeanne Ripley

ALL THE OTHER PHIL THOMPSONS ARE DEAD

Such a Neat Idea
Took my "Whale Poem" to Rick Rofie
brought tears to his eyes

I thought it was the poem
but his best friend
poet Phil Thompson
born same month and year as I
drowned the day before
wading to his Nova Scotia island

Rick printed our poems on opposite pages
the dead and the living for better or worse
stapled together for posterity

Twenty years later
on my Nova Scotia island
sitting on the bottom of this half dug well
I smoke my pipe on my 40th birthday
watch swirls of spirit smoke
spin upward
past drying leaves
and think of dead Phil Thompsons
wherever they might
not be

In Yellowknife, back from vacation
I open the newspaper
and find another Phil Thompson died on my birthday
after a life of service to aboriginal people
and left a scholarship fund in Native Studies

Should I send a cheque?
Or apply for it myself?

All the other Phil Thompsons are dead

TALL TIMBER

Shake hands with the planet
bury the hatchet
make your peace
fool
or fortify the barricade

Eat, devour, gulp
lick, pick, peck
drink like a fish
you buffoon bonehead
flathead, meathead, marblehead
knucklehead, jackass
boob

At least your forefathers
had foresight

they saw the alien future
the tall timber
forsaken

oblivion foretold

THE FENCE

Early I climbed
the triple-barbed wire barricade
casting long shadows
in the autumn morning

Like a soldier
in midday matinee war movies
over the top
to where the wind blows free
and seagulls soar
by the harbour

The fence is still there
protecting armed forces children
from unsupervised exposure to nature
But twenty years later
I learn to leap
beyond the rusted barbs
designed for soldiers
and children
trained to be soldiers
who changed their minds

CHRISTMAS TREE WELCOME

Nova Scotian balsam fir unfolds
thawing in our Yuletide livingroom
uprooted like the audience
the tree sips sweet water
and makes soft crackling sounds
as thirsty branches reach for warmth

This nourishment cannot replace
the spirit soil of coastal hills
three thousand miles to the east
where images of ocean still breathe
through needles evergreen

Lobster boats slice the Gulf Stream fog
Osprey dive to reach flat calm
and rollers crash on mountain rock
sinking into restless sea

This is your final sacrifice
— to come from where
we want to be

Welcome
Welcome
Christmas tree

THE COMPOSER

for Pete Stokes

The composer sets
meticulous musical flame
under hand-forged words
of poetry

He tempers the text
with fire and steam
so lung bellows of a choir
ignite
the audience

and melt the poet's heart

SURFER

Still living in the adolescent Sixties
the green neoprene wetsuit manboy
drives a rusted metallic cave
to the ultimate pacifist beachhead
and waits for the wave

Like a windcrest never breaking
always moving
he catches anything he can ride for free

To be his friend you must ride with him
or be just another wave
he sees
paddles to empathetic speed
and captures
coasting on your energy
until the crash
the foam on the rocks

The surfer always bails out before the end
but through stinging eyes
you see him stroking
short practised thrusts
to where the waves begin

SEAGULL VORTEX

Above this island earth
warmed by hot sun
surrounded by cool Atlantic blue
a dozen seagulls rise
on the thermal of my breath

Some circle one way
others another
But none of them flap
their wings like me
still stuck here on the ground

DANIEL ASLEEP

Seashells, mussels, and pieces of crab
line the round red table like a fortress

The bag of marshmallows emptied on the embers
Today we rode the big waves
engine straining through the channel
and when the spray soaked your jacket
you just laughed
full of joy

We chopped, dug, watched, fished, cleared
swept, talked, sat, carved, poled and climbed
this day away

Listening to the wind
the faraway cars on the mainland
watching squalls roar across the water
from the top of Goat Rock
I am moved to love you
more than my words allow

WHERE JOSEPH HOWE ONCE SLEPT

This vision
of your weeping mate
tips scales of passion
back to balance

Absorbed by your ocean-blue eyes
sharing the wine bottle
watched by tugboat captains
I stumble
freefall toward the harbour
cutting my hands on rough ice crystals

Cold wind
not yet spring
the dying tree has fallen
but there are no seedlings

Years later
your sculpture of a cresting wave
on the waterfront
and my memory
of our first meeting
in a house where Joseph Howe
once slept

WINGBEAT EYES OF GOD

Wild geese fly south
over Jasper Lodge
where elk graze
the lush September tourist lawns

The geese see
a 5,000-year-old map
Each melted setback
of the Columbia Icefield
since the glaciers

They see and remember
the crusade of time
Locked in a V formation
the heartfelt ancient vision
of the wingbeat eyes of god

RIDING BEFORE THE STORM

High clouds darken the previous sky
Horsetails gallop after my old VW van

But the old engine endures
smiling at memories of 160,000 miles
blowing exhaust in the face of the storm

Quick stop: liquor store for coffee liqueur
Rush through for groceries: steak and eggs, beans
winter cabin food

The storm closes in to witness
the legal separation of sun and earth
citing marriage breakdown
the adultery of clouds, a conspiracy of snowflakes

At the boat, the wind gusts to forty knots
waves are huge, snow-whitened
the wind blows fiercely in my chosen direction
only fifteen hundred feet of moderate swell
riding before the storm

Balanced for a high aft, the old rowboat testifies
as a character witness for her builder
She does not swamp
But it's days like this I always wish
the oars were the same length
and I'd remembered my life jacket

Biceps hurt and gunwales strain
to deny allegations of rot

The southwest cove is calm, my cabin warm, wind sheltered
and on CBC radio they tell me traffic is all tied-up

Civilization has been cancelled
and they don't even know I made it

Heart Strain

Fresh oranges explode memory's refrigerator
The morning sun lances this page
and I wonder where I am

When the juice woke me
I was back with my grandfather
in a small coastal village

He rose early to cook a hearty breakfast
like he had for the crew
of the *Venture* three-masted schooner
lost before her time
lost in the month of my birth

I was the boy sailor
to be taught lessons
of ocean and nutrition
before the school bus came

DON'T WALK TOO PROUD
YOU WILL MAKE ENEMIES

EAT AN ORANGE EVERY DAY
SMOKE AFTER BREAKFAST

BE QUIET IN THE WOODS
OR YOU WILL HEAR NOTHING

LOOK TO THE SKY FOR WEATHER
NOT TELEVISION REPORTS

DO YOUR CHORES. DANCE. SING.
FIGHT ONLY WHEN NECESSARY

KEEP A CLEAN GALLEY
READ A NEWSPAPER EVERY DAY

Thirty years later
the juice of fresh oranges
brings him back to me

No Law in Pelly Bay

151 proof rum
to protect against polar bears
we walk the cold gravel
beyond the limit of the law
in Pelly Bay

A dry community
the wet ones have RCMP
and domestic crisis centres

My friends sip the over-proof rum
to soften the wintery September wind
and fill my Pepsi can
again and again
with this Arctic Circle initiation

No law in Pelly Bay

But last year a community elder
found fondling
his granddaughter
ceased to exist
shunned
until his brains faded away
in the bright light
of his shotgun

No law in Pelly Bay

After hearing this story
I became the man who crawls
and sings sea shanties
between ramshackle Inuit houses
until the Regional Director
helped me to my room

SCOTT-FREE

Armed with Yellowknife booze
you returned alone to Rankin Inlet
just in time for the party

In the blizzard
people huddled in a duplex
where I imagine you flirting with eager Inuit girls
longing for their dark eyed love
to fill empty spaces
left by three sons and a wife
on Prince Edward Island

When thick smoke cleared the building
in the confusion, the screaming
the icy genesis of fire
you helped everyone to safety
and then went back for more

You missed work for the first time
Monday and Tuesday
They organized a search party
checked your bachelor apartment
and declared you missing

We know where you are
now — sleeping in the frozen ashes
They found you curled up in the utility room
looking for someone who already escaped

Your final child support payments:
A lesson in courage
for your three sons
a fat insurance cheque
for your ex-wife

And you got off scott-free

TRAPPED

The telephone rests on green carpet
beneath hanging ferns
Pine bookshelves and buff brick
warm the livingroom wall like a fireplace

Curtains are open
Rain on the redwood balcony
Beyond, the grey sky is still

There is no one home in the new modern apartment

A black and white cat walks from the kitchen
licking her lips

She has been alone for five hours

A spider crawls
horizontally
across the wall
four feet from the floor

She jumps
catches
eats
touches down
then goes to the window
to watch seagulls flying

The telephone rings

She spins around
body steeled, ears erect
swats the receiver from the cradle
before the second ring

and listens
to the surprised and unknown voice
She would answer if she could

AFTER THE LAWYER'S MEETING

Parked
silent
Sackville Street
after the lawyer's meeting

Separation agreement
tactics
strategy
matrimonial property rights

The war escalates
but all I want is peace.

Ferryboat bounces in the harbour
dwarfed by idle oil rigs

The sunshine hurts
my windshield

Down the street
a class of children
hold hands
in the custody of women

They parade by the old van
and smile at a man
who reminds them of their father

The daycare staff
pull them back in line

They will make certain
they never get to know him

WHALE POEM

One time it was men
and their dories
who struggled
like so many playthings
in the frothy wake
of his escape

They were gnarled men
and strong
of spirit and mind

There were even times he felt
they deserved
his blubbery pelt

But no more

Now they kill
with dynamite-loaded harpoons
cutting cruelly
tearing ruefully
deep

And no proud leap
beneath glistening stars
to the tectonic bars
of the music
pounded out by his heart
can rid the whale
of the modern whalers

Though they may soon
rid our earth of him

COLD ROSES

Toronto flower girl
keeps her petals fresh
in the freezing wind

You can see her
by her cart
as you look down from the CN Tower
over a bowl of Maritimes chowder

See her speck
of warm human dust
below phallic metal towers
where taxi drivers
think Halifax
is a fishing village

And poets
sell cold roses
to keep from going sane

VASECTOMY

Cutting remarks
snip masculinity
with sneering technology

So much easier for the man
she said

But what if there's a holocaust
and I'm the last male?

Imagine
thousands of surviving women
wanting me
needing me
to continue the species ...

What if they knew I had a vasectomy?

You don't have to tell them
she said

DUCK PEACE

Gray sky low-cloud morning
ice-crusted spruce and fir
faded dark green
frame the marsh view

Flooded spartina grass punctuated by Goat Rock
a six metre glacial boulder
patched with driven snow
commands the wave-rippled saltmarsh
like a full moon

Moving slowly the descendants of duckbilled dinosaurs
conduct their ancient mating dance
of bill thrust and wing flap

Dozens of black submarines
with moving conning towers
enjoy the ceasefire
the silent guns
the empty blinds

But at the edge of the narrows
where tide pulls the melted floes
a flock of whistling wings explodes
when the eagle dives

Flapping hard the great bird drags
his daily meal to the frozen shore

SHOTGUN POEM

Powerful at short range
scattered at a distance
ideas often missed their target

Wild birds seeking freedom
on tireless heartbeat wings
whistling through salt marsh air

When eye and hand
triggered
the perfect trajectory
he could pull truth down
wounded
from the blood-red morning sky

And when love
circled back
to defend her mate
he could not take aim
or set her free

FISHERMAN BLAKE

We motored over for a visit
in your old aluminium boat
sealed with white lightning
rivets leaking

Cruising through the August marsh
my sons laughed
as your Cape Islander's wake
bounced our small craft
like a fairground ride

Lazy Tide has served you well
and carries a modest morning sea harvest
back to dock on a kind afternoon

They had never seen such fish before
Thirty pound cod!
How could you lift them?

We fed the guts to gulls
talked about fish prices
limited markets
and my 30 days at sea
on the big trawlers

You threw us the haddock
because it goes bad so fast
and sprayed the boys
with your cleaning hose

For someone
who doesn't like to socialize much
fisherman
you have given us
a special moment
captured in memory
by the gills

TOO MUCH PRIDE

Lost two good teeth Friday night
at Captain Todd's Tavern
Musquodoboit Harbour
Nova Scotia

An unemployed fisherman
baited my mouth
with his normally productive fist
and left bits of white ebony
strewn on the red carpet

Guess he thought I had
too much pride

Sitting here in the early March
solarium trapped sunlight
with a black turtleneck
and toothless grin
I feel the cool earth chill my legs
and the bright rays draw my spirit
like a spring flower

The balance of the universe:

Life rises from death
with too much pride

THREE CANDLES

Three candles churn
the midnight cabin air

Each for a son
snuggled in the sleeping loft

The heron squawks
over the moonlit bay

These candles cast
your father's shadow

But the flame
belongs to you

PEOPLE GOTTA EAT

I clearly remember spring
driving to George's farm through mud-filled roads
trying to collect his seed payment

Night. Full moon rising over the back-forty
Cold. Quiet. Frosty as the task itself.
I close the car door, walk to the farmhouse kitchen

"Where's George, Thelma?" She looks thin
more nervous than usual

"Up on the hill with the team ... been there since daybreak ...
ploughin's gotta get done ... people gotta eat!"

I say goodnight, refuse her offer of hot coffee
and plod slowly through the sweet fresh field
half man, half horse ploughed

George will be seventy-four next week
His organic shadow seems to furrow the moon
as the team pulls in my direction
We meet at the crest, he yanks the lines
and steam breath of horses mingle with his
in the midnight air

"Evening Maurice, s'pose you want the seed money?"

I stand humbled by the smell of good earth sweat
awed by his capacity to work
the irrelevance of the Depression to his infinite worth
and I clearly remember
his massive hands groping deep in overall pockets
for handfuls of pennies, nails, wire, tobacco
sugar for the horses glinting in the moonlight

"Gotta get my work done, Maurice, people gotta eat!"

He turns, snaps the lines, disappears over the crest

A modern banker would call his loans
sell the horses for glue, leave the farm vacant

But treading back to the car
with his image etched on my mind
like a sculpture
I resolve to buy his seed myself
for as long as he lives

People gotta eat

BELOW FORTY

Below forty
skin gets crispy

earlobes bite
the beard crusts

you want to hide in exhaust pipes
of running cars
and sleep in a deep heap

you will do anything
to keep from walking into the wind
without longjohns

but the best thing
is that you don't have to convert
from Celsius to Fahrenheit

and like turning forty
you're the same distance

from absolute zero

STONE-COLD BABY

When the unnamed woman died at ninty-two
doctors found her baby calcified
dead in utero
unborn for sixty years

My grandmother had a stillborn once
The nurse tried to take it from her
without a goodbye

but she sent the nurse away
and gently dressed
her baby daughter
in a crocheted shawl

then she held the stone-cold baby
to her heart

and sang the hardest lullaby

THIRTY/TWENTY VISION

Insidious fibreglass particles
the wounds of looking too hard
too long
plucked from my eyes
Doctor said it was rare
for vision to improve
from 20 to 30
and when I read the bottom line of his chart
he said only a few
have 30/20 vision

Feeling the wet sidewalk with my boots
watching minuscule droplets spatter
into the future
I felt relieved my environmental commitment
years spent in people's attics
had not made me blind

Loving the unexpected power of vision's gift
I turned my eyes to the world

Ice glistened in late November treetops
on Oxford Street
secret hints of streetlight rainbows
sparkled where no one else could see

Faces of children in faraway cars
spoke to me of hope, fear, confusion
The slightest wrinkled line
a raised eyebrow
heard clearly
as the rustle of wind

Then a man with a white cane
asked me for directions
but until I closed my eyes
I did not know the way

HE DANCES ALONE

They were going out dancing
the night they broke up
He told off her friend
She wouldn't come home
so he packed all his things
and slept in his car

Now he dances alone
but not in a bar

He dances with room to move
and the sound of the wind
through her chimes

He remembers old katas
and moves like a warrior
with the heart of a poet
until tears turn off the music

But her windchimes
will not be still

GRANDFATHER'S LOBSTER TRAP

Well, they took away the licences, you know
The family fished for lobster more than 200 years
Smelts too, and eels speared blindly through the ice
anything, so we could survive the depressions
we hardly noticed anyway

> He rowed further down the inlet
> where the rush of breeze on the salt marsh
> felt like angels saying shhhhhh

Don't know why the government has to screw everything up
They killed the Merchant Marine, frigged up my pension
and while I was away fighting their bloody war
on the Atlantic and the Pacific
the bastards took half the family land for taxes
Jesus

> The side of the boat made soft, creaking moans
> bending to the strength of his rowing
> He threw his makin' smoke over the side
> and asked me to tell him
> when we were over the hole

So I guess I got a right
to take a lobster or two every year
licence or not
seems fair enough for all I gave them

> We pushed the trap over the side
> where the biggest lobsters hide in Petpeswick

> Then, because the wind was right
> we stood in the boat with jackets held open
> and sailed slowly back to the narrows
> like a two-masted schooner
> laughing as the sun sparkled off shells so brightly

> It seems like only yesterday

HOUSE ALONE

House alone
one side
the gravel road
other flanks
have fir trees
curved on top
the way wind blows

Forest and unpaved road
go on forever
stopping once in a while to chat
with cities
and oceans

Inside the house
grandmother scrubs everything
she cleaned only yesterday
and waits for the mail

See her face
by the kitchen window
Hear the wood stove sing
the only song she knows

THREE THOUSAND MILES

Three thousand miles to the west
it's six in the morning in Halifax
My eyes sore
from miles of aching highway
some turns like Canada
others foreign

So many people and cities
Such age
I long for freshness in the countryside
a pioneering spirit
Germany, France
too many war movies

Everywhere I look
bullet holes
craters
trenches gentled by the hands of seasons
hordes of soldiers marching in the twilight
intertwine with the sunset
leave a presence

Half my ancestral roots
were severed here
Uncles breathed their last here
for podgy politicians

This place
this crippled humanity worn place
this Europe
is not my home
but we have earned a part of it

Rainbow's End

Morning screech of tires
wakes the herons
our dog barks
as the crash of metal on wood
shakes the Petpeswick peace

I rise before the sun to see gulls circle
like vultures
across the main channel
Call to the tree-hidden accident scene
over a half-mile of marsh

"Does anyone need help?"

A neighbour finds not a mark on her
this young mother of two
on her way to work at 6 AM
Did she swerve to avoid a deer?
They say there were tracks

Later
a rainsquall describes the prettiest rainbow
three full rings, six colours deep

and where her family gathers
surrounded by flowers

the rainbow ends

THE TRUCKS

The trucks are going again
we hear them
sound waves surfing through the trees
riding a dense fog
where are they going at 1 am?

Anonymous in the mist
their lights disguise illicit cargo
toxic chemicals
to illegal dumps on the Eastern Shore
lumber destined for bankruptcy auctions
seized bales of marijuana

Invisible
they sail down the midnight highway
cultural ghost ship time capsules
to be treasured by archaeologists
when found in future glaciers
perfectly preserved fossils
with CB radios intact

OLD CHARLIE LEAVES THE TAVERN

Move slow
Charlie
legs like old grey molasses
tottery and unbalanced
yet every move sure as inflation

The blind man first receives
your aged embrace
touched by the knowledge
you too will soon see nothing

Hug the waiter like a brother
Charlie
caress his biceps
with your wrinkled map of wrists
that lifted Alberta hay bales in fall
and Yarmouth lobster pots in spring
for most of the century

Leave the tavern
Charlie
wave goodbye to your only family
and forget the pain
of your faraway grandchildren
who never write
but call sometimes
to ask for your furniture
and war medals

November Nuance

When I parked the car by the old grey dock
the boat was gone
You moved her, cousin, to the point
hauled her up and flipped her
because the weather turned cold
and you didn't think
I'd come to the island until spring

The wind rises from the southwest
warm for November
carrying acid rain from New England

Muscles flex the rowboat from her winter cradle
and down the slip
Let the wind blow her to the car
walk the bowline through the dormant coastal marsh

Tethered and beached, I fill her with supplies
chainsaw, oil, gas, food, life jacket
and check car windows against the predicted storm

Rowing into the wind I aim across the tide
sit far to starboard to keep from swamping

Think now of the pace of my life
Pull, stroke, rest, correct
and my seafaring grandfather
dead six years
who left me this island
softly beckoning through the mist
and a legacy of unforgettable summers
treating me like his only son
who had forsaken him for another coast
five thousand miles to the west

BUREAUCRAT

Spoiled child darling
white-haired boy
cringe
grovel
cower
curry favour
(*see* servility)

Tremble like a leaf
wince
shrink
shiver in your boots

Your position
is surplus

CANADIAN ODYSSEY

High Level Quick Lube
sperm me, baby, sperm me
John Boy Full Service
across from Our Place motel

Welcome to Improvement District 22
Our committee met for five years
to accomplish this sign
We left most of the trees
wrecked, rusted cars
and this dusty road to Peace River

Give me the discipline of cruise control
set, coast, accelerate and resume
Drink red wine at Stan's in Thunder Bay
beside the Sleeping Giant
Stella's round table at the Prince Arthur Hotel
Stop to salute the statue of Terry Fox
put a blanket around his shoulders
to keep him from the cold rain
Wildcat crosses roar near Wawa
while I drink Wildcat beer with my wild woman

On the 401, Toronto folks enjoy
forcing out-of-town plates off unchosen exits
Handicapped ramps for disabled drivers
used to dirt roads and wood buffalo
with better manners
In Yellowknife we carry rifles in our trucks
for drivers like these
so they stay in Toronto where its safe

Our bear totem plates covered with Fort Providence dust
won't wash off after three thousand miles of rain
A New Hampshire family wins a bet ...
there ARE bear plates!
They get our address and my tape of the Gumboots

Quebec City — *Je Me Souviens*
Our room in the clouds looks down
on a misplaced Halifax Citadel
This time the French saw us coming
armed with VISA cards
We drank white German wine
and later on a king-size bed
went supersonic
at the Concorde Hotel

Paradise and surrender
on the Plains of Abraham

Driving across the Tantramar border marsh
singing along with the music
of Rita MacNeil
we hold hands
under the dark clouds
of home

LURES

The fisherman whips
the soft line
to dry in the autumn wind

He sets it down lightly
a silken thread
on cold black water
to drift like a twig

Cast your glance
to the snow-covered rocks
Set it down lightly
on the white powder

Your eyes are those of the fish
and the fisherman

There are lures everywhere

INTO THEIR HEARTS

Trees felt it happen
wars scarred their collective memory
for ten thousand years
But this was different
no mud-filled trenches dug
no hand-to-hand combat
just one flash of psychic energy
blasting through the universe
to be sensed by living things everywhere
eons into the future

The speed of light is slow
and life rare
trees know this

Though many died hundred of years before their time
outside the target cities
most lived on

And when our survivors came back to them
to build small shelters
beneath guardian branches
trees sucked the poison air
into their hearts
so the children below might live

MOUNTAINS DON'T PRETEND

Mountains don't pretend
to be anything else
They just sit there
looking rather mindless
and let men decide
how pretty they are
or try to get up
enough faith
to move them

Dynamite would be better

People are good at destroying things
that don't pretend to be
something else

Imitation would be better

PATHFINDER

Hitchhiking back to the city
December, almost sundown

Traffic too neurotic near the bridge
so I walk the catwalk
where someone else has gone before

Deep in the ice-crusted snow
his footprints are dark holes
I plunge my feet into for easier walking

The wind blows hard and cold
nearly drowns the sounds of cars

I tighten my hood to look down at the river
which seems too far below
for even summer swandives

Halfway across the footprints end
beside a pile of clothes

Frigid from the morning rain
they are rigidly stacked
like plywood on steel

Vision blurs at the loss of my companion
Tears freeze in the wind

Was he really a stranger?

Although not a Christian
I carve a cross on the crusted snow
and observe a moment of silence
at 10° below

On the way to the police station
it is much harder to walk
without his footprints

EMBERS

Wood crackles
woodstove embers are like memories
glowing life rings unfold
red-tinged
as their seasonal skin
heat peels away

And the trees lifestory
flashes before our eyes
in a burning white glimmer
of stored summer sun

Listen
we can hear long-dead birds
sing again

Fire is a time machine
like the melody hummed softly
recalls other songs
links us to all music

Here
in this timeless harmony
sit by the renewable fire
and join all
who have been warmed
by the spell

ON PHOTOGRAPHING A POET

for Lesley Choyce

Sun drenched scrapyard
searching for the re-invented wheel
among rusted lyric hulks
where teenage dreams
compete with gravestones

Closer to the light
that filters down
through dappled trees
my fingers caress the camera
some say wielded better
than my pen

Here
you are framed by the window
of an old surfer's Ford

There
you contemplate
the dewdropped spare tire
long ago discarded
by an upwardly mobile lawyer

Composing the poetry of your young face
the dynamic tension
of elitist sentiment
and simple fisherman philosophy

I wonder if you believe
this jock photographer
with karate damaged hands
can care enough

[click]

to love you like a brother

EIGHTY-NINE YEARS

When I sat by the psychic
in K-Mart Mall
for 15 bucks
he told me
I'd live eighty-nine years

This was worth every penny
since I always expected to die sooner
and have insurance pay my debts

He told me I lived in great tension
between art and science
and thought I must not give up either
but try to find balance
and stop looking at my watch
start paying off my loans

This left me wondering
what it will be like in the year 2040
when right on cue
I fulfil his prediction
and breathe one last breath
marked by the line
at the base of my right thumb

So if I fibrillate before then
and contort my chest
do not call the paramedics

Phone the psychic

Tell him I want my money back

BE YOUNG AGAIN

Be young again
stand with both legs taut
straddle the leather seat

The bicycle is new
but your body has deteriorated

Your face is known to summer winds
and by them changed

Wheels spin and air,
stewed in harvest seasonings,
whooshes by as though you stand
where sea cliffs join and end
behind Cape Blomidon

Tribal chieftain kneels at power's edge
inhales moist rumblings of wind and tide
draws energy
inward

In the city, yank on the handlebars like a 10-year-old
ride on the sidewalk
Pedestrians cough politely
as the chain falls off

Traffic lights fade from red to green
the path to your camp lost
in the darkness of no moon

Many tribes have come this season
hunting has been good

Lift the alloy-blue machine up steps to the apartment
pass through the door
and hear the skins of the teepee
rustle softly behind you

AIR

Air is not particles of matter
mixed gaseous state

This is not air

Who told you that?

Why do you believe it?

Air is cleansing freshness in the chest
when you haven't had any for a while

Fingers of hair
that would've stayed put
if it hadn't been moving

Deep alto moans of telephone
and power lines
when storms use their orchestra
against us

An invisible pillow outside your car
you can rest your hand on
at 60 miles per hour

What you compress
and take with you for company
on scuba dives

What whales stay awake all their lives
to breathe

CHESS BY MAIL

Concentration lures
our unseen shoulders square

and the pieces move our fingers
as though distance and time
were pawns to the queen
of the moment

Sometimes I see you
behind different pieces
on the other side
of our continental chessboard

Mountain air cleanly flows
into my lungs

Coyote calls freeze
in the moon wind

In this longest of games
I send postcards
of sailing ship dreams

You give me crisp
non-bureaucratic
mountain poetry

Held freely by the ebb and flow
of these ancient patterns

We can both only win
my brother

Peace be to thee

Pawn to queen three

THE PARTING

When we marry
the community gathers
to witness our vows

Old ladies, aunts, uncles, lace & cigars
Everyone comes to share
the new love

But when we divorce
lawyers pucker their expensive lips
sneer their bank accounts
to Everest heights
and teach us to hate
to slice our worldly goods
and lives asunder

No one comes to our parting

No one wants to hear us say
we'll always love each other
but can't stand the way we squeeze
 toothpaste

No one wants to see us remove
wedding bands and pass them
to our children dressed up special
hoping to change our minds

THE CABIN IN WINTER

Morning comes
we're living inside a fridge

the radio batteries are frozen
and yesterday's coffee
a brown stone

the orange saved for breakfast
does not bounce

the woodstove is asleep
and windows are frosted
like stained glass in a church

You tell me
underneath your army surplus
double-down sleeping bag
the emperor has no clothes
and that it's my turn
to start the fire

Soon the tide will shift
the inlet ice
like continental drift
and we will be stranded

The floor makes exploding sounds
as I hop holding my cheap sleeping bag
rigid from the night's early sweat
and with my axe
try to break the ice
in the bucket of water
for our kettle

THE *ELLEN FLETCHER*

Side-trawler out of Petit-de-gras
first two weeks at sea
as a Fisheries Observer
Storm came up
we were full of fish
radar out
Mate asleep at the wheel
when I noticed she was rolling sluggish
Slid down the ladder to the engine room
seawater right up to the deck
Pumps were out
We were sinking
Woke up skipper Ray Malloy
he jury-rigged some pumps
and saved the ship
Said I could sail with him anytime
But it was the spirit of my great-grandfather
Gustav Solberg, Master Mariner
who lost a trawler off Cape Breton
in the Twenties
he saved the ship
I just used his Norwegian instinct
for self preservation

Old Houses

All cities have old houses
where no families live

Layers of paint like growth rings of trees
determine their age

Entire groves of them
clear-cut every year
by lumberjack developers

They are where young people go
when summer's gone
Row upon row
line the tattered pavement
looking like poppies
in someone else's poem

If they could flap
their inner wooden tongues
modulate timber bowels into vowels
they'd speak about children
wandering through the night
like dilated pupils

With staring glaring panes
they'd look at you
with honesty guaranteed
by old age
and say how the sunrise
has lost it's splendour

JACOB'S POEM

At age four, Jacob gave everyone
in his life new names

Daniel is Thunder
Shawn is Lightning
Jacob is the Sun.
His mother is Trees
Pat is the Ground
Jennie the Road
Mike, Houses
the dog, Schooner, is the Light

and me, his father, he called Ice
because I moved to Yellowknife

I now note with wonder
that the Sun always melts Ice
comes after Thunder and Lightning
helps Trees grow
warms the Ground
sheds Light
sometimes sets on the Road
and shines on Houses

Ice on the other hand
Falls from the sky
during Thunder and Lightning storms
freezes branches of Trees
protects the Ground from winter
makes Roads slippery and dangerous
hangs from the eaves of Houses
reflects the Sun
and dislikes untrainable Light

Jacob summarized our lives
in nine words I can't explain
in forty years or lines

MOCHA

Curled beside the highway
she looked asleep
except
her bloodied tongue
hung on the gravel
tasting death

Tamora Mocha
Chocolate Labrador Retriever
child of the Beothuks
bred to survive icy current
not 40 mile per hour
fenders

You first swam at ten weeks
jumped out of the boat
in Petpeswick

And never bit a child's hand
no matter what they did to you

At the Maritime Writers' Workshop
we shared a van for a week
and you heeled by my side
without a leash
and heard Eli Mandel
tell me I was a great poetry editor
and to apply the skill
to my own work

Even in death
you let my sons touch your rigid body
and helped them understand
that no one
is invincible
to tears

LOST IN OTTAWA

Lost in Ottawa among early spring egos
we drive to the Gatineau Hills
to search for flowers you knew as a child

You promised to teach me to be literate
I gave you frisbee lessons
a slightly used sweater
and a piece of my battered lifeguard soul
nearly drowned by eager nonswimmers
but afloat

Earth time mountains
Yes, I'm still an unwilling Virgo
contaminated too rarely by fire

See the way to the river
my wineskin
a trusting doe
scents us from the other bank
where we plucked the flower
of friendship
and sowed the seeds
of losing touch
by touching

SEA OF SLAUGHTER

for Farley Mowat

So quiet here
the birds are gone
impaled by risks
of human garbage

Only wind
sings

No wingbeats
or feathers for our caps

PENUMBRAL MOON

Steeped in fear of self and other
we watch this slowly wobbling world
defy our warnings
embrace the dark time precipice
of this penumbral moon

Our crystal union of kindred spirits
could weather heat
loss or gain
retain the edge
hard polished by a soft path destiny

Souls felt the barometer rising
saw silent eyes
of peter principled policymakers
heard the blank stares
of oil rig workers
driving Cadillacs

Our childlike innocence
like a flower crushed
by passing limousines
learned we could not change the world
ten years before her time

Let us raise our children in peace
until the stars agree
our day has come
one way
or another

I WILL MEET YOU

I will meet you in this place again
the softly falling rain
will not deter me from my aim

Streetcars may evaporate
with the cooling hand of time
and pavement may demonstrate
all the failings of our lime

The days may pass with swiftness
as the years slip fast away
but our tears adapt to richness
as the night awaits the day

See the flaming bridges
that we've scattered through the past
watch the ragged edges
as they try to mend too fast

Look for brazen reason
when the moon is bright with dust
capture every season
without a need for lust

Hold beneath your sorrow
these truths I've tried to say
for sometime after tomorrow
there will surely come a day

When I will meet you in this place again

DISTANT MEMORY

We are imprisoned by the phases
of a circle moon
snow moon
wolf moon

My footsteps are nearly silent
as the train whistle beckons
from a tunnel built by prisoners
two centuries ago

I can smell their sweat and hear songs
see hot soup passed around
behind hedges of time

Fence me in
Don't fence me in ...

Change hands on the whip
time master
be discreet

We see the lay of the land
the diffuse moonlight
spreads our perimeter
and our enclosure defines
a turning point

Show restraint with the belt
Do not punish me

As the wind blows
in the natural course of things
I have only the moon
a pen
and someone else's
distant memory

ON THE ROAD NOW

He slipped almost warm fingers
into his ragged gloves
and spoke to me of strangers
and syncopated doves

I wheeled the old truck over to the curb
pine tree boughs rasped
on the breeze
but the night seemed relatively at ease

He stepped into the autumn wind
his hair blew wild and free
I asked if he'd return again
he said he didn't know where he would be

He buttoned up his rawhide jacket
and grasped his time stained case
wished me fare-thee-well
but I couldn't see his face

I offered further help
and a place by our hearth
out of the rising storm

He said it would be warm
but I'd done enough
and he was alone
on the road now

I pulled away sadly and with care
not to throw a stone
and saw through my mirror the hitchhiker
who was my only son

Acknowledgements

Joe Blades — for enjoying my poems as much as I do his, working hard for all of us, and for helping to pick the title for this book.

Joyce Thompson — for marching off to school when I got detention for writing my first poem, and for the joy of song and dance and always working hard to help others.

Glynn Thompson — for showing me strong men can be kind, and for selflessly dedicating 50 years of his life to the love and support of his wife and family.

Gertrude Bayer — for crossword puzzles, knowing "Danny Boy" at 91, and showing me how to hear pure joy in the songs of little birds, and see it in the leaves of violets.

Luther Bayer — for teaching me strong men can be passionate, boxers can be dancers, that you must fight fair to win, and for leaving me this island to pass on to my sons.

Maxine Gruber — for teaching me to type at ten, and that women can fly float planes.

Janet Rathbun — for sharing the joy of bringing three sons into the world, for loving them ever since, and for ten of the best years of my life.

Lesley Choyce — for letting me help him get into Canada to become one of the most productive writers I've ever known, and sharing the joy of starting *The Pottersfield Portfolio.*

Patricia Travis — for being my best sailing partner ever, a great step mom to my sons, and for the highest courage in the face of personal tragedy I have ever known.

Jeanne Ripley — for being my true friend through two of the most difficult years of my life, forgiving my confusion, and reminding me of my own wisdom.

Jayne Ings — for encouraging me to send this Mss to Joe Blades, and for teaching me, if only for a while, to sing from the heart.

Colin Cameron — for teaching me you can still value yourself after mistakes, that everyone needs time to play, and best friends stay close in the hardest times.

Wayne Thompson — for being such a good listener, wise counsellor, and brother, and for making up a thousand songs in thirty years without worrying about writing them down.

Glynis Thompson — for loving poetry all of her life, being my best sister, and for ordering lots of copies of this book on the Net.

Scott Thompson — for showing me oldest brothers aren't always the best songwriters.

Pete Stokes — for finding hidden music in my poetry and adding better music of his own.

With respect and admiration for my three favourite Maritimes song poets — Lennie Gallant, Stan Rogers and Bruce Guthro — for their enduring fusion of poetry and melody.

A Selection of Our Titles in Print

96 Tears (in my jeans) (R.M. Vaughan)	0-921411-65-0	3.95
All the Other Phil Thompsons Are Dead (Phil Thompson)	1-896647-05-7	12.95
Best Lack All, The (Tom Schmidt)	0-921411-37-5	12.95
Coils of the Yamuna (John Weier)	0-921411-59-6	14.95
Cover Makes a Set (Joe Blades)	0-919957-60-9	8.95
Cranmer (Robert Hawkes)	0-921411-66-9	4.95
Crossroads Cant (Mary Elizabeth Grace, Mark Seabrook, Shafiq, Ann Shin, Joe Blades (ed.))	0-921411-48-0	13.95
Dark Seasons (Georg Trakl; Robin Skelton (trans.))	0-921411-22-7	10.95
for a cappuccino on Bloor (kath macLean)	0-921411-74-X	13.95
Gift of Screws (Robin Hannah)	0-921411-56-1	12.95
Heaven of Small Moments (Allan Cooper)	0-921411-79-0	12.95
Herbarium of Souls (Vladimir Tasic)	0-921411-72-3	14.95
I Hope It Don't Rain Tonight (Phillip Igloliorti)	0-921411-57-X	11.95
In the Dark—Poets & Publishing (Joe Blades)	0-921411-62-6	9.95
Invisible Accordion, An (Jennifer Footman, editor)	0-921411-38-3	14.95
Like Minds (Shannon Friesen)	0-921411-81-2	14.95
Lad from Brantford, A (David Adams Richards)	0-921411-25-1	11.95
Longing At Least Is Constant (Kathryn Payne)	0-921411-68-5	12.95
Manitoba highway map (rob mclennan)	0-921411-89-8	13.95
Memories of Sandy Point (Phyllis Pieroway)	0-921411-33-2	14.95
Milton Acorn Reading from More Poems for People. (Milton Acorn)	0-921411-63-4	9.95
New Power (Christine Lowther)	0-921411-94-4	11.95
Notes on drowning (rob mclennan)	0-921411-75-8	13.95
Open 24 Hours (Anne Burke; D.C. Reid; Brenda Niskala; Joe Blades, rob mclennan)	0-921411-64-2	13.95
Poems for Little Cataraqui (Eric Folsom)	0-921411-28-6	10.95
Railway Station (karl wendt)	0-921411-82-0	11.95
Rant (Sabrina Fowler-Ferguson)	0-921411-58-8	4.95
Rum River (Raymond Fraser)	0-921411-61-8	16.95
Seeing the World with One Eye (Edward Gates)	0-921411-69-3	12.95
Song of the Vulgar Starling (Eric Miller)	0-921411-93-6	14.95
Speak! (Jim Larwill; et al)	0-921411-45-6	13.95
Speaking Through Jagged Rock (Connie Fife)	0-921411-99-5	12.95
St Valentine's Day (Jennifer Footman)	0-921411-45-6	13.95
Strong Winds (Sheila Hyland, editor)	0-921411-60-X	14.95
Túnel de proa verde / Tunnel of the Green Prow (Nela Rio; Hugh Hazelton, translator)	0-921411-80-4	13.95
Under the Watchful Eye (James Deahl)	0-921411-30-8	11.95
Unfolding Fern (Robert B. Richards)	0-921411-98-7	3.00

Order from **General Distribution Services**, 325 Humber College Blvd, Toronto ON M9W 7C3, Canada: Toronto, ph 416 213-1919 ext 199, fax 416 213-1917; Ont/Que 1-800-387-0141; Atlantic, Western Canada, NW Ontario 1-800-387-0172, Telebook (CTA) S 1150391, customer.service@ccmailgw.genpub.com ; USA 1-800-805-1083, gdsinc@genpub.com , Pubnet 6307949. Sales representation by the Literary Press Group of Canada, ph 416 483-1321. Direct from the publisher, individual orders must be prepaid. Canadian orders must add 7% GST/HST.

BROKEN JAW PRESS
BOX 596 STN A
FREDERICTON NB E3B 5A6
CANADA

www.brokenjaw.com
jblades@nbnet.nb.ca
tel / fax: 506 454-5127